The House on Cross Street

FOREWORD

This book is a compilation of memories, both tragic and heart-warming, from my childhood in Anderson, Indiana. Growing up in North Anderson with several generations of my family along Silver Street, I developed a foundation of strength, sense of pride and belonging, as well as a natural gravitation toward responsibility and learning.

I want to express my appreciation to every person who was a part of my upbringing as we are all products of our family, friends, neighborhoods, schools, teachers, classmates, coworkers, education, and experiences. Social construction plays a monumental role in forming our sense of self which is in a constant state of evolution. We are always growing and changing just as this manuscript did from the day I started putting my thoughts into words on May 31, 2001. It began as a way to simply contextualize my life experiences and begin the healing process. It culminated with internal peace and understanding through the growing years of sporadic writing, endless edits, and long days of painful thoughts.

I want to especially thank Toni Shoemaker, my 11th grade Creative Writing teacher from the original Anderson High School, who graciously volunteered to edit the final product.

To Jolie and Brandon, I could not be more proud of the adults you have become and our closeness that has grown over the years. Mom always wanted us to stay together which is why I chose to move in with you. I knew you would need me, and I certainly needed you.

To my best friend Janet Rowland and her mother Betty Rowland, I want to thank you both for being my family. While I had the desire to succeed within, I could not have accomplished anything without having the opportunity and encouragement you provided once I moved to Bloomington. I knew how things like going to work, paying bills, and saving money was supposed to work, but it didn't in my life before I became a part of your family. I have great respect and admiration for both of you.

To my maternal uncles, aunt, and cousins, I thank you for the examples you set for me in my early years with grandma and grandpa. You instilled a sense of family pride and belonging within me that got me through the hardest times.

To my paternal aunts, I know that I am a painful reminder of the brother you lost. I am grateful you always tried to include me as part of the family.

To my all my close friends who were with me along this journey, I could not be the person I am today without you as we are all connected in one way or another. Just as Clarence says in my favorite movie *It's a Wonderful Life*, "Strange, isn't it? Each man's life touches so many other lives."

CHAPTER ONE

Our Mom

You can never prepare for it. You can never honestly say that it's going to happen, no matter how grim it seems. I tried to prepare myself that it could happen, but I don't really think I believed that deep inside. But on Sunday, June 25, 2000, in a small extended care facility in Indiana, it did happen.

It was a place that was supposed to help get her life back on track. It was a new beginning. At least that's how I saw it. It's what I wanted to believe. She hadn't even spent two full days there yet. She was uncomfortable there for many reasons. Mainly, I think it scared her to be 51 years old and surrounded by people that were clearly in worse shape than she, or so it seemed. I sure wouldn't want to see myself in that environment when I still have half a lifetime to live. She was in slight pain from the feeding tube surgery, but that was expected. Her new roommate was an older woman who was probably suffering from Alzheimer's. I didn't even have enough time to get acquainted with the woman's family. Time. Now, that is an interesting word. It sounds so infinite. I always catch myself saying, "I didn't have the time" or that "time just flew by." Then suddenly, without warning, you wish you could have made more time somehow. You wish you could make time count for something. She was probably thinking about her time, all of her past years, as she laid there- wondering, waiting, worrying. Her life was now in someone else's hands. That's ironic, I guess, because my mom's life had been in someone else's hands for the past 30 years or so.

I thought it would be a nice place- rustic, peaceful. I had hoped that she would find it a good place to begin again. She had always talked about southern Indiana, especially since I had moved here eight years prior. I know she wished she could have just gotten up one day, packed her belongings, and headed south. But like I said, her life was always in someone else's hands. Her life was not her own. She was a prisoner in my hometown of Anderson. She had never been away from there for more than overnight. She never felt like she could get too far away. She wanted to though. I could see it in her eyes every time I saw her. Desperation. I could see and almost feel it. I found it becoming increasingly harder to leave her there, but I didn't have a choice. I kept telling myself that it was her life, that she was an adult and could change if she wanted to, that she must like living that way. Those were lies I told myself to make it easier for me to drive away. I knew she didn't have a choice. She was captive there, and I could not change it.

I would only see her twice a year, even though it was only two hours away. When I would visit, I would have her come out to my car because the stench in the house was too powerful. She lived in such deplorable conditions that I wouldn't have let my cat live there. When you see that kind of deterioration in someone you love, it's almost unbearable. My mom's life had been reduced to a single bed in the middle of the living room floor, covered with a filthy comforter and sheets, in a home belonging to an ex-husband. Her belongings consisted of what she could keep in old dirty purses, hidden under a pile of clothes that was stacked higher than the bed. The clothes were from Goodwill or the local thrift stores. She called them her "good clothes" as though she couldn't see the stains and rips, or smell the stench from the house on them. She had close to ten suitcases that were packed with more of her "good clothes" stacked in the corner. She also had old silk flowers from previous weddings packed carefully away. Although the husbands were long gone, she held on to the remnants of those days as though the men in her life were meaningful to her. The marriages were always sad failures for one reason or another. Her prized possession was an original black velvet Elvis painting bought for her by an old boyfriend. I could see that all she wanted was that fairytale wedding where there was love, honor, and respect. I think my mom only found that once in her life, but that had a tragic ending long ago.

Mom was homeless, even though she lived in a house. I would have rather seen her in an actual jail cell than living with her boyfriend, in her ex-husband's house. Her ex-husband, Larry, had a good heart, but living with my mom could try anyone's goodness. They had a strange love-hate relationship. He took as good of care of my mom as anyone had in the past. To be honest, he just couldn't get rid of her. He tried changing the locks, but she would break in through a loose door or window frame which wasn't hard to find. He would then say nothing else for a week or so, and then would try it again. She had a lot of fire and fight in her to say the least. A survivor. She knew she didn't have anywhere else to go. She had some type of control over him, and I think he was just plain lonely. I even took her to the local hotels to live with her boyfriend, but he would track them both down and move them home again. I use the word "home" loosely because it was not anyone's idea of an actual home. You could say their home life was like a daytime talk show that drags people in from the bottom of society to capitalize on sad lives. Mom would call the police because she said he tried to kill her. When the police would show up, mom would be throwing things at him, and he would answer the door naked. It was never-ending. Part of the problem was the paranoia that was setting in on her mind. I remember she called me absolutely hysterical one day. She frantically explained that he put bleach in her bath water and on her washcloth so he could kill her. In reality, I know that mom never drained her bathwater. Our bathtub always had to be scrubbed and sanitized before we could use it. After the water sat for hours the remnants of dirt and soap scum would cling to the tub. Sometimes she would even put the dirty dishes into the tub to "soak" because there were so many of them. Larry probably had decided to clean the tub not realizing she had not gotten into it yet. It was not unusual in her last years for her not to bathe regularly so, in his defense, he might have just been thinking the water was from her last bath. Explaining my theory to her was a lost cause.

CHAPTER TWO

Grandpa

Mom had not held a job for as long as I can remember. She would dispute that fact, but it's true. She wasn't as full of ambition as most of her siblings: a sister and three brothers. She was the fourth child of the five. My grandfather was the strong patriarchal type who took care of everyone, including the neighbors, their kids, and anyone else who needed it. I never saw him without a half-smoked Roi-Tan cigar in his mouth, sometimes not even lit. I always thought his dark flannel shirt and blue work pants smelled from the stale smoke, but I loved to be with him. He worked 3rd shift at one of the two GM factories, the heartbeats of the town, and worked on washers and dryers on the side. If someone needed money and all they had to sell was a dryer, he bought it. That's why we had three or four working washers and dryers lined up the concrete garage wall. My grandmother never had to wait to switch laundry loads. She would be out in the cold, cluttered garage all day doing laundry. She had an old baseball bat that she would use to force the clothes down into the washer. I don't think she trusted that the washer would actually suck them down into the murky water. She was always yelling at grandpa to clean up the mess out there. There were smelly rusted tools, useless gadgets, and parts for cars that were no longer made. There were old Maxwell House coffee cans filled with nuts and bolts sitting on every shelf, in every corner. It was like an old forgotten tool shop, but grandpa knew the location for anything he needed. It was a two and a half car garage, but no cars or trucks would fit in it. It was kid's heaven, but an old lady's nightmare. She fell quite frequently, and it scared her to be out there alone. He slept during the day, so if she did fall, no one would hear her. He had many hiding places out there. He would occasionally sip on his Windsor whisky, and then tuck the bottle away. I found many bottles out there as I rummaged through the treasures. Some empty, some half full, some forgotten. Grandma was always looking for them and would ask if I had seen any. I think I lied about knowing where the bottles were most of the time. I didn't know why he didn't keep the whisky in the small garage refrigerator with his beer. I hardly ever saw him drink beer except on baseball nights when he would sit in the kitchen corner with his transistor radio on, with the old white ear plug in his ear.

Grandma's TV time could not be interrupted for anything, day or night. It was long before a television set could be found in every room of a house. They eventually were given a small black and white set for Christmas that was put in the back of the kitchen on a shelf. Grandpa could then plug his ear piece directly into the TV.

I guess I knew why he drank. Living with grandma and dealing with her sisters when they visited would have made anyone drink. It scared her not knowing if he had any drinks before he left for his night shift at the factory. Looking back, I know now that she thought he was always drunk when I think his blood sugar was just low. He would sometimes sit at the table eating his supper very slowly with his eyes closed. He had been diagnosed with diabetes and grandma said that made him drink more. I never knew of him to miss any work. He never complained about being sick. I didn't know about his heart condition until the day grandma woke me up for school and said grandpa couldn't breathe. It was 6am on November 7, 1980. I was eleven. He had sat at the kitchen table all night, not wanting to wake anyone up. She was used to him being gone at night so it wasn't until she had gotten up that morning and saw him. She told me to go across the street to my friend's house until the bus came and go to school. Defiantly, I told her "no," and ran to call my Uncle Tim. I knew he was the closest to our house. I barely caught him before he left for work that morning. I told him something was wrong with grandpa and that he needed to come. It seemed like only seconds when he arrived. I don't remember talking with grandpa that morning, but I would not leave until I knew what was happening with him. The paramedics arrived and made him walk out to the ambulance, through the front yard. We never went out through the front door, always the squeaky back door in the garage. There wasn't even a sidewalk to our front door from the street. Silver Street. It was the lot of the old house that had long ago been torn down to make room for the new one. I watched them walk him though the yard, holding onto his arms. He always held onto grandma's arms, but no one ever had to hold his. I watched, but he never looked back. As they all left, I went across the street as I had been told. All of the neighbors were out that frosty November morning, watching. Most were relatives that had never known any other neighborhood. I called my mom and gave her instructions to come quickly. I promptly informed the neighbors that I would be waiting on my mom to pick me up, *not* going to school. I had always been quite independent and was much older than my biological years. I finally did walk to their house because I was scared but would not openly admit to it. I watched out the window while I waited on mom and tried to be strong. I didn't know what was happening since nothing like this had ever happened before. As mom drove up in what seemed like hours, I ran out and told her to drive me to the hospital. She was afraid that she wasn't supposed to take me, so we waited until she found out if we could go. It always seemed as though she never did the right thing according to the family, so it wasn't unusual for her to wait to be told what to do. After several hours and several crying fits, I started out walking. I knew the way. I had gotten down Silver Street to the house that Aunt Sadie, grandma's sister, had built years ago. Knowing my determination, she finally picked me up down the block and drove me to the hospital. I didn't know then that I would be making that same trip again in a little over a year.

I walked in the front doors and immediately smelled that plastic, antiseptic hospital smell. I saw all of my uncles and aunt sitting with grandma. They were all quietly crying to themselves. I walked in and told them to take me grandpa as if I were in charge now, but I was told that he would be out soon. Uncle Tim was just coming out from seeing him. He had apparently told the "boys," my uncles, to take me home and he would be there soon. I watched the direction from which my uncle had come and kept wondering if I could make it to the doors without someone stopping me. After a short while I decided that making a run for it would be useless. A doctor appeared finally appeared through the silver swinging doors. He walked to us and began to speak. I watched and listened and looked at everybody's expressions trying to make sense of what he was saying to them. They were all holding my grandma. I looked over to another door as I heard Aunt Nancy scream "No!" I wanted someone to tell me something. What was happening? The doctor said "unresponsive." What is that? I wanted my grandpa right now. I was grabbed and held by everyone so tightly I could not breathe. Even if they hadn't grabbed me, I don't think I would have been able to breathe. I just wanted my grandpa. It was 11 am. He had died of congestive heart failure, and my life was about to change.

CHAPTER THREE

<u>Silver Street</u>

I would go with grandpa on weekends when he had to make a service call to someone's house. At four years old, I would actually diagnose a worn out agitator on the phone when people would call. I never knew if I was actually right or not. It became natural for me as his assistant to try to help when I could. Of course, I knew more about the appliances then than I do now. He took care of us: my mom, sister, brother and I. He even paid most of the bills when mom was married to my step-dad. I actually lived with my grandparents, but my siblings lived with my mom and their father in a house on Cross Street, which was only a few blocks away from my grandparents and me. Our old, tree-lined neighborhood was full of relatives for at least two streets. The house I lived in was the same that my mom had grown up in, as well as some of her siblings. It had been built by grandpa after my mom was born. Their first house had been torn down to make room for the new one on the same lot. The house was made of concrete block. It wasn't the most attractive house, but it was built to withstand anything Mother Nature could send its way. The window frames were metal and somewhat moldy from the condensation that had formed over the years. The blocks around the windows were usually moist. The floors were always hot so I had to wear socks, even on the dark blue speckled carpet. Grandpa had run copper water pipes under the floor to keep them heated when he built the house. I knew where every hot spot on the floor was so I would run and jump over them.

I thought our yard was huge, the biggest in the neighborhood. There was a slide in the yard that had belonged to grandpa when he was a boy. It was a black park-size slide, not just a store bought slide. No one else anywhere had one like it. There was a red rusted swing that he and grandma would sit in at least once during a hot summer evening. My basketball goal was tied to the end of the swing frame. I spent many hours practicing to be a basketball star, my first career aspiration. A Harlem Globetrotter to be exact. Sometimes, during one of those summer evenings that grandma actually came out of the house, grandpa would drive me up the road to the railroad tracks, across from the old brick school he and grandma had attended, walk me through the wildflowers in the ditch alongside the dirt road, and talk with me while my ear was against the rusted rails. He had shown me how to listen for trains that were still miles away from our old family neighborhood. He took me there several times each summer just to listen and talk. The old school had long ago become apartments. Now, it is just a vacant lot. I doubt that anyone that lives in the neighborhood now even knows that the old school even existed or that is was the foundation of the that neighborhood. After all, it had provided the means to educate all those who would grow up and start their own families there. Like everything else, time had changed it all. Time.

Grandpa did the grocery shopping on his way home from work each morning. He would stop at the little store down the street, then called The Ranch, and pick up whatever we needed. I always liked going to the store with grandpa on weekends. He would stop and talk with an old man named George, who always smoked a pipe. George was always standing there, with his black suit on, white shirt, tightly cinched black tie, and dark gray suede dress hat as if he were on his way to church. It didn't matter what day it was, he was always there. He would puff on his pipe and smile at me while he talked with grandpa. I don't know where George lived, or if he had a family. Maybe he was a school pal of grandpa's. I never asked. I wish I would have. "Pal." That's what grandpa called me. "Pal." And I was his pal. During the colder months, he would always pick up a bag of peanuts on his way home from work. He would come in with warm, fresh donuts from Dunkin Donuts and wait until I was ready to leave for school. After I had my favorite white powdered, strawberry crème filled pastry, we would be on our way. The first stop was North Anderson Elementary to pick up a few of my friends. He would then drive a couple of blocks to Shady Side Park, where my mom had married my step-dad a few years earlier, to feed the squirrels. My friends and I thought this was the best thing ever as we tiptoed across the fallen leaves in the park trying not to crunch them under our tiny feet. Feeding the squirrels on crisp fall mornings. Who would think that this would etch a permanent mark in a memory?

I only saw grandpa cry one time in my life. One cold winter morning, after getting home from work, unloading the groceries, and giving me the warm donuts, he went back outside to start the mint green Jimmy again. One of my little white kittens, Snowball, had apparently climbed under the hood to get warm. When he started the engine, the fan belt, well, it was too gruesome to see. The tears poured down his rough whiskered cheeks as he held me so that I wouldn't go outside until he had mustered the strength to clean it up. Grandpa had gotten me several kittens over that summer and fall, much to my grandma's disapproval. Somehow, they all ended up dying unexpectedly. The first was Tiger, a gray tiger kitten, whom I found under the grape vines. Then there was TJ, Tiger Junior, who I found the same way. Next was Snowball, the kitten who was trying to get warm. Snowflake, Bo and Daisy all ended up dying. Snowball was the only explainable death. I am sure my grandma had something do with it, since she despised cats to no end. Grandpa probably didn't even know or he wouldn't have kept getting me kittens. The dogs he got me somehow all got loose and ran away. She hated dogs, too.

My grandpa actually grew up in the house next door to the concrete house that he built, and my grandma's original house was behind his, before Pizza Hut replaced it. The Wiseners owned grandpa's old house for awhile, but eventually moved to the next street. I used to go knock on their door just to say hi. Mrs. Wisener would come out to the porch and talk with me. Even after I moved away, and they moved to the next street, I would stop to see her when I was in Anderson. Next to his parents' old white house, with the standard black shutters, was his sister Thelma's house. It was a small house under huge shade trees that always kept her yard muddy and grassless. I can remember that her husband, who looked like Adolph Hitler with a brown cigarette in his mouth, was always building a basement of some sort. You could see underneath their house. It had been like that from my earliest memories. The house was dark and had an odor. I wasn't allowed to go in her house, but I never knew why. I think grandma said I would fall through the floors because she had covered up the holes with throw rugs. I don't know how grandma would have even known that. She never came out of the house, let alone travel down the sidewalk two doors down.

Uncle Garland, grandpa's brother, lived across the street with his wife Alberta and their poodle Pepper. Aunt Itha, my grandpa's aunt by marriage, lived several houses down from Mrs. Whitaker's on the other side of the street. I would ride my bike down to Itha's and help her clean green beans from her garden during the summer. Itha was married to Charlie. His hair was whiter than any hair I had ever seen. He was tall man, but not as friendly as Itha. He mostly just walked around the house or yard, without ever saying anything. Mrs. Whitaker seemed to be about a hundred years old. She always had her white hair in a bun and wore pretty sky-blue homemade dresses. She walked every day to the grocery store across Broadway with a little cart. Every Sunday morning she walked down the alley to the church when the bells began to ring. And every afternoon she worked in her small garden. I had never been in her house, but being the friendly type, I would go knock on her door weekly just to say hello just as I had done with the Wiseners.

The nurse from Dr. Blassaras's office, Mary Layton, lived kitty-cornered to us. Her husband was the brother of my grandma's sister's husband, Lester, but I didn't know that until I was older. They had a son who was married to my step-dad's sister, too. Their daughter, Carol, was one of mom's best friends. Mary walked every day to work and would say "hi" to me on her way home. Next to her was Mrs. Johnson's. They say that Mrs. Johnson was a black lady, but I never once saw her. Not once in the eleven years I lived on that street. Her front porch was covered with a huge overgrown pine tree. I don't remember anyone even visiting her. The house across from Mrs. Johnson's belonged to the Mendenhall's. Apparently, my grandma's sister Sadie had built that house before she moved to Florida. That was before my time. I only knew of Dorothy Mendenhall and her family living there. I would visit Dorothy as she worked out in her yard every day. Her son had a big basketball goal and sometimes she let me practice there. They lived next to the Abstons, who moved in after Kenny Smith moved to Kentucky. Grandpa took us there to visit one time. We found Geodes in the yard, and I took home a car load of them. I thought they were real treasures that I had discovered. Kenny actually moved back to Anderson after his wife passed away. He then married one of my grandma's sisters, Florence, when he came back. Everyone said they would be able to take care of each other. Most of Kenny's fingers had either been amputated, or maybe he was born that way. I never knew. Aunt Florence had her legs amputated from bone cancer, so I thought they did make a good match. I liked Kenny, but didn't think too much of Florence even though she was the one related to me. She was always yelling like grandma. I think she was the one my grandpa disliked the most out of all of grandma's sisters. Although, grandpa really didn't care too much for Aunt Bessie either. She was a short, stout, bossy woman who couldn't see over the steering wheel of her Nova. The old psychic medium on the original Poltergeist movie bared a very close resemblance to her. She tried to slap me once for imitating the Hee-Haw raspberry that Roy Clark and Buck Owens did on the Saturday night broadcast. I must have spit on her by accident, but I was just singing like all of the people on the Saturday night shows: Pop Goes the Country, The Porter and Dolly show. It seems it made grandpa so mad that she tried slap me that he went out to get a switch off the tree to smack *her*. She never tried that again, even though I'm sure grandpa never really hit her with it. He liked switches, or the threat of them. He used to chase me around the yard with one occasionally when I wasn't minding. I think I got stung on the back of the legs by one or two, but he didn't catch me too often.

Next to Uncle Garland lived the Stanley family. It was a huge family and it took me years to know all of their names. Their grand-kids would come over when they were visiting and play croquet with me, when grandma let them. Grandma wasn't too happy with kids hanging around our house. She would always tell me that she wasn't watching anybody else's kids, and they weren't watching hers. She didn't quite understand that kids just played with each other, and it wasn't like a baby-sitting job for the parents. Mom ended up marrying one of the Stanleys, Larry, in her sixth or seventh marriage. He used to always ride his bike in the rain or snow through our neighborhood because he couldn't drive for some reason. I probably even threw mud balls at him from the puddle at the end of our gravel driveway as he rode by the house. I don't think he drove until he married mom. He was the ex-husband with whom she was living with her boyfriend before I took her away from there.

Most of houses in the neighborhood had been occupied at some time or another by family. The yards were well kept, but not landscaped and chemically treated like yards are today. The spring always brought out the dandelions and clover, but no one was in a rush to kill them off. The houses were tidy and clean and had nice people to take care of them. There were always birds chirping in the trees, and butterflies fluttering through the yards, especially on the wild honeysuckle that grew along our house. Grandpa taught me how to open the honeysuckle to get the sweet juice out. As you walked past the huge freezer in the garage on your way out the door, the subtle fragrance of the honeysuckle overpowered the grease smell from the garage from the old car parts. Spring days always smelled like wild honeysuckle there. On the outside, everything looked picture perfect as it probably had since the end of World War Two. It was the ideal working middle-class neighborhood thriving from the post war boom. The factories were making lives easier with stable jobs and household products of convenience never before seen. I seemed to have the perfect childhood, in an old perfect family, in the old perfect neighborhood. But on the inside, mom wasn't perfect. She was already on a path that would eventually lead us to a life of poverty and take her to her death.

CHAPTER FOUR

The Call

"Ms. Watkins?" I replied "yes" to the voice speaking to me that morning. "I am sorry…" My mind went numb before she could finish. I couldn't breathe. I had to get up from bed. I looked at the clock. 6 o'clock a.m. She continued to say "your mom passed away in her sleep this morning." I was in shock. I started pacing around my bedroom floor, arguing with her. I said that there had to be a mistake, that she had just been there two days, and that the doctors said she would make it. I told them her name and asked them to check again. The soft patient voice just assured me that there had not been any mistake, and she was very sorry. I hung up the phone, took a deep breath, and held back the tears. I couldn't cry yet. I had to make phone calls that would change lives forever, like the one I had just received. My first call was to my brother, Brandon, who was staying near the facility at my girlfriend's house while she was out of town. He was only home on a weekend leave from Ft. Leonard Wood, Missouri to spend some time with mom. He had been coming home for the past few weekends to see her while she was in the hospital. The phone rang but he didn't answer. I kept thinking that if he could go to the nursing home, he would call me and tell me they were wrong. I thought maybe they had moved her bed or her chart or anything. I then tried to call my sister, Jolie, in Denver. I had to get a voice on the phone so that I was not standing there alone, shaking. No answer. By this time, my thoughts were getting more jumbled. I had to take a deep breath. I tried my brother once again. A tired voice answered. I firmly instructed him to get to the nursing home since he was only several blocks away. He was a little disoriented from a call so early in the morning. I finally to him was able to tell him that they had called. "Mom died," I uttered. "What?" he asked in disbelief. I repeated myself even though I knew he had heard me the first time. I told him that they said she had died in her sleep between 4 and 6 o'clock that morning. I didn't even remember the patient voice telling me that, but I was repeating it to him. I told him I would be there within 30 minutes. I then called my sister and felt I could no longer be composed, even though I knew I needed to be calm for her. I took a deep breath instead of falling apart and made the call. A part of me wanted to wait for just a few minutes so that Brandon would call and say it was a mistake. A part of me, however, knew I just needed to make the call to my sister so that she could get home. This time she answered. "Jolie?" Another tired voice replied "yeah." "Mom died this morning!" She screamed out, began crying, and asked what happened. I told her that I just had gotten the call and didn't know anything yet. I told her I would call her back in a few minutes. I then called my partner who was on vacation in Florida. I could not hold back any longer. When she came to the phone, I began to cry. I told her that I would call back with more details in a few minutes, once I got to the nursing home. I made calls to my aunt Nancy, my mom's boyfriend, her ex-husband, and her closest friends as I tried to pull myself together to drive.

The twenty-five minute drive felt like an hour. The sun was fresh and bright over the rocks along the highway that Sunday morning. There were very few cars. The drivers that passed me had no idea of the struggle I was having trying to drive. The tears kept filling my eyes and my heart wrenched from the invisible knife that was slicing through it over and over again, tearing the muscle to shreds. I looked at the rock formations along the roadside and thought about the last drive I took with my mom just two days before. We talked about how the layers of rock had formed over millions of years in the depth of a great ocean. She, like me, had always been intrigued by strange trivia about the Earth and the people on it. The conversation we had almost resembled a mother-daughter talk about our lives, the future, Christmas. I can't really remember any talks like that from the past. Talking with mom was more like a shouting match. Neither of us ever won our argument, but we both wanted the last word. Mom could go off on a tangent about things that happened years ago. Senseless things that I thought had been settled. Things over which I did not have any control but somehow felt I was to blame. Jolie and Brandon ended up in the same type arguments with her. It wasn't just my rebellious teenage know-it-all attitude that provoked them. Mom would get so mad she would start to spit as she yelled, which infuriated me more. There wasn't any yelling the morning that I drove her to her new temporary home, what would be her last home. It was calm. I could tell she was nervous. She kept asking if everything was going to be okay. I assured that she would be home for Christmas and that we would all be together. I promised her that our family would be a real family again, even though we were never a real family.

I can't remember the last family Christmas together. Mom wasn't much on cooking a big Christmas dinner or keeping holiday traditions. Our lives were too chaotic to even get excited about Christmas. Most of the time, the three of us arranged to be at our friends for Christmas Eve and Day. It just saved us from disappointment. We never knew when mom would get up from bed to start cooking for the day or if there would even be food to cook not to mention if there would be clean dishes to eat from. That time of year was never the same after grandma and grandpa passed away. Christmas Eve used to be the greatest night of the whole year for me. To this day, I still try to make Christmas time the way I remember it, but it never is. The entire family, including cousins, girlfriends and boyfriends of cousins, step-relatives, and neighbors of family members would all gather at the Maxwell house. Anyone that showed up could expect a gift. For days before the grand night, Grandma and her sisters began making peanut butter fudge and divinity and putting into tins for any unexpected guests so that everyone had a gift. After grandpa passed away in November of 1980, then grandma in December of 1981, everyone faded away. Everyone broke off into their own family units. That's where my family branched off into our friends' family holidays and into our own personal hell. It was just never the same. I know it upset mom, but she never had the strength to get everything together. I thought by promising mom a great family Christmas, it would give her hope to cling onto.

We all think that she knew what was coming for her. Mom had been in a serious and dangerous state of depression for years. For that matter, I barely remember her not depressed. There were a few times in our lives that it didn't seem so bad. Those times were long ago, when Jolie and Brandon were little. Mom loved drinking Pepsi. I can almost see a long glass bottle in her hand when I think about her. She would open a bottle and start playing her cherished Elvis albums or Johnny Lee's *"Lookin' for Love"* record. She still could not believe Elvis was gone. She was one of those who believed a great conspiracy was involved to fake his death. Mom would dance around with us, laughing, re-living her younger days of sock-hops and juke box nights at the local milkshake shops, Frisch's, and Jumbo. It embarrassed me mostly, but looking back I wish I could see her dance just one more time. She seemed really happy when she was dancing, drinking Pepsi, and listening to the King. I always thought mom lived in the sixties. She wore bell-bottom jeans until the late 80's, ten years past the trend. That embarrassed us too, until she started wearing the super tight jeans, but by then big jeans were the fad. Mom was always had her own unique personality quirks. She didn't care what other people thought, not even us or the other parts of the family. She was certainly the black sheep. I think part of her didn't want to be like them. I guess if I had dealt with the tragedy she had in 1969, I would be stuck there in that era, too. That was the year that I was born. No, I wasn't the tragedy, although sometimes I felt that way growing up. I think she blamed me for the some of the bad times in her life. Maybe she didn't blame me. She was just envious of me for living with grandma and grandpa. I had everything I needed there when she was struggling with Jolie and Brandon to survive.

CHAPTER FIVE

<u>1969</u>

It happened in October that year, 1969, just three months after I had arrived on the historic July 16th moon launch. My dad, Bob, was killed in a car accident early one morning on his way home to his parent's house. The details have been obscured over the years so I don't know that anyone really knows what happened. Mom would say after one of our screaming matches that I was not an accident, that I had been planned so that she and my dad could get married. He was already trying to get a divorce form a previous marriage, but it was messy as they usually are. He was only 22 years old, with two daughters. I have a half-sister out there somewhere that I never knew. I only met her once when I was around eight years old. I believe my great aunt Ludy and great uncle Charles on my dad's side took us camping in Alexandria. That was the only time I saw her. My parents felt that if mom was pregnant, the Maxwells would allow her to marry him once his divorce was final. Mom said that it was supposed to be final in January 1970. I have read his letters to her and know that although they were just kids themselves, I was a planned event. They loved each other. It was a time when young women were supposed to have children, a working husband, and stay at home. Mom would always tell me that's all she ever wanted from life. I guess that could have been why her ambition for a career was so low. I also know that she desperately wanted out of my grandparents' house. I have been told that mom was an unwanted child, and my grandmother never let her forget it. Grandma was a sharp- tongued woman who yelled most of the time. Don't get me wrong, she took wonderful care of me. But the screaming was a daily event. Mrs. Wisener told me after mom's death that she could hear my grandma calling my mom horrible names through closed doors and windows. How a young girl could have done so much to be called a streetwalker, an old term for a slut, I'll never know. But then again I wasn't around yet. My turn came around, but I don't think it was as bad as mom's experiences with her. Combined with an unhappy childhood and a young love to sweep her away, my mom jumped at the chance to get pregnant and start her adult life. Her hopes and dreams were cut short that October when he hit a telephone pole and was trapped in his truck. An explosion occurred and there wasn't a chance for him to get out alive. The newspaper said he was burned beyond recognition, with legs and arms burnt away. It made the front page the next morning. I think she always lived with that in her mind. Who wouldn't? She said that she got phone calls warning her not to bring the bastard child to the funeral. Mom knew who made the calls but would never say. She was forced to live at home, but now with a child. She was nineteen at the time. I really believe that mom's problems started in adolescence, but her shot for a family of her own was once again only a dream. As I got older, when she still gave me birthday cards, she would write the same things: "your dad would have been proud of you", "you were planned", "we wanted you." I wished I could have felt those things, but I never knew him. It was hard with all of the screaming to feel those feelings from her, let alone from someone who had died before I even knew what he looked like or knew what it was like to be held by your father. She began taking pills that summer, to get her through the pain. Unfortunately, that pain would last another 32 years and so would the pills.

Mom did remarry. She had another shot at happiness. I was three years old when the event took place. I don't know much about her meeting the future father of Jolie and Brandon. His name was Tom. I'm in the wedding pictures, but most of them were lost due to mom's transient living. Grandpa didn't like him that was for sure. If a psychologist could have a made a case study of the two of them and their life, the outcome could have been predicted. Tom was a quiet man, until he started drinking. He could quickly become a mean bastard that wanted to destroy anything in his path. He was a blue collar worker, mostly getting employment at gas stations from what I remember. I know that he missed a lot of work, which is why grandpa paid most of their bills. Sometimes grandpa would come home, scratching his bald head, puffing on his cigar like a chimney, and shaking his head is disbelief. Mom was certainly not prepared to become a mother of me, an adult with responsibilities, or a wife of an anti-social man who disliked work. Jolie and Brandon suffered the most. They would steal my toys when they came to grandma's house because they had very little. I remember that I always thought they were so dirty, with dried food around their mouths and stains on their clothes. I was six years older than Jolie, seven years older than Brandon. I really just didn't like them. I thought they smelled of stale cigarette smoke. Grandma would always send home groceries with mom, and grandpa would give her money. I was happy when they left, although I usually had to call mom to tell her to bring the stolen toys back once I took inventory after they left. I was a spoiled grandchild. I guess my one aunt and three uncles felt sorry for me since I didn't have a dad, or a mom that didn't meet anyone's approval. I was smart. Probably too smart for my age. Mom would say not too much later in my years that she was the mom, not me. I picked up on what I heard everyone say. Since we were an old family, I had great-uncles and aunts every week in the house visiting. I heard their comments about my mom. I tried to ignore most of them because she was my mom, the only one I had except for grandma. My teenage cousins Vance, Jeff, and Joe would come to town and take me to Dairy Queen, to play basketball by the North Anderson water tower, or for drives in their cars. My aunt Nancy would take me to the Best Ever ice cream store on Broadway next to Shadyside Park for vanilla cokes. They never went to mom's for Jolie and Brandon. Looking back, I can see how dealing with mom was challenging, so my family just stayed away. They could not have just stopped to visit because she would have demanded money for groceries that would have been used for pills. I can see how all of this upset mom, but it was out of my hands.

CHAPTER SIX

Cross Street

When I was five, mom asked what Tom and I did when we were in the basement together. I didn't realize that I was about to deal her another blow. She was in the second bedroom of the house where she and Tom lived. She was pregnant with Jolie. She was painting the room yellow and hanging Raggedy Ann and Andy pictures from Home Interiors. I was playing with my Hot Wheel cars on the wood floor as she worked on the room. She had already bought a new yellow-orange patchwork bedspread for the room she had hoped Jolie and I would share someday when we were a real family. I only visited on weekends then, but I knew she wanted me to live there with her. She asked me once what it would take for me to move in with her and be a family. I replied that she had to divorce Tom and get cable television. I had to watch Saturday cartoons without lines through the picture. Moving the manual antenna around was not my idea of a good Saturday morning. I would only go with her after my morning line-up was over. I had tried calling Tom "dad" once, but it just wasn't right. I never called anyone dad before, and I didn't realize then that I would never in my life call anyone that name. I told her that he did things. She asked what things. I began to recount the details she wanted. She stopped decorating and sat down with me. I don't how long we talked nor do I remember any expressions. I then took her to the musty basement to show her a towel that he kept in a box. It wasn't there. Tom built model trains sets. I explained that he would lay me down on the plywood of one of his train sets, remove my panties and raise my shirt, and proceed to use his hands and fingers all over me. I told her how he would use his mouth on me. I explained in great detail how I had to use my mouth and hands on him. At the time, I thought all kids did this for their fathers, and I just wanted to be good kid. Somehow though, I knew it would upset mom. I'm sure it was because Tom always stressed the fact that it was only between him and me. He especially drove into my mind that my grandparents must never know what we did together.

I can still remember the musty smell of a damp basement. I can feel the cold train tracks on my back. I can still hear the creaking wooden floor boards from above. It was my job to listen to the floor so see if mom, who was at home, would get too close to the basement door. After all, it was a secret between just him and me. Naturally, I wanted to please him, do what I was told, and not let him down. Although I'm sure it started before they lived in that house, it was in the basement on Cross Street that my memory became stained and my senses became heightened. It didn't end for close to seven years later. I don't remember the first time it happened. It was just something that always had happened. It had always been a part of my life. I didn't know any better yet, it made me upset and ashamed. I estimate that it happened for at least seven years, on and off, when I visited. After they divorced, he would still come to town and stay with her. If I happened to be there, she would leave me with him. He always made sure he touched me and made me touch him. Nothing had changed even though they were divorced. One occasion I remember well is shortly before they divorced. Mom was home and Tom was in the shower. I was probably eight or nine years old. Tom called me into the bathroom. There was not any shower curtain so water would always be all over the floor. Tom had soap all over him. He told me to use the soap on him. I never even understood why this was important to him. I didn't understand sexual pleasure then. He would always tell me when I would complain that whatever he was doing hurt, he would say "it'll feel good in a minute." But it never did.

It seemed like every time we were in the car alone, he would pull me close to him. He would put his hand inside my pants. He did this frequently when he was taking me back to grandma and grandpa's after a weekend with mom. Somehow I knew even at such a young age, Tom was a very disturbed man, and so child-like when he was doing these things to me. There was a time when he came in from a night of drinking while they still lived on Cross Street. By this time, Jolie and I slept in bunk beds in "our" room. He stumbled into the room through the darkness, trying not to wake mom. He once again put his hand in my underwear. I grabbed his hand and told him to stop or I would yell for mom. Somehow I had undergone a transition from feeling that this was just something fathers did with their kids to knowing something just wasn't right about what he was always doing to me. That night I think I was afraid that Jolie would wake up and know what he was doing. The thought of that enraged me, and for the first time, I was able to tell him to stop as though I was the adult and he was the child. He immediately stumbled off to his room. Jolie told mom when she was about three or four years old that when she was sleeping between them one night on Cross Street, she opened her eyes and saw the devil at the end of the bed staring at her dad. It scared her so she closed her eyes. When she opened her eyes again, the devil had moved to the side of the bed, but was still staring at him.

After the day that mom asked about what she already suspected, the topic was only mentioned two other times. I always bore the burden that I knew something that would kill grandma and grandpa, since Tom kept telling me that. It was a big load for such a small child to carry. I had what we called "sock fits" every morning before school. The seams on my socks across my toes set me into a rage. I also had what the doctor called a "nervous stomach." I was put on nerve pills to help calm me. Obviously, the secret caused the outbursts and stomach issues. In second grade, I was so sick with vomiting and diarrhea, diagnosed as colitis, that I missed school for what seemed to be a lengthy time. The principal of the school watched our house from the alley across the street thinking my grandparents were just not sending me. He finally did come to the house to see if I was really sick. My grandma woke up my grandpa to speak with him. I don't remember the exact words, but grandpa told him to never come to the house again.

When Tom got home later that day after it was confirmed what was happening, mom confronted him. He was getting the Chips Ahoy cookies out of his dresser drawer. He usually hid those from me as though they were his secret little stash. I always knew where they were, but never wanted any of the cookies anyway. I never understood why he had to hide cookies. Mom was telling him about the day and the conversation. He looked at me, said I was lying, and that was the end of it. He got mad and left the house. He came back though, for about 5 more years. Mom never mentioned it again during that time period. She took me to what I thought was an Intelligence Test a few days later. I had to draw pictures of the "family." I can remember that I always drew male figures with beards and mustaches, like Tom had. I also drew the family, the one I wanted, as the man, wife, and child all holding hands like the other families I had seen. Like all of my friends' families. I found out later, years later, that the psychologist, not the IQ tester, determined that I felt no fear from Tom since I included him in all my pictures. He had told mom that the pictures depicted normal family relationships so I must be lying. No one ever asked why I had drawn those pictures. If they had, I would have told them it was the family I wished that I had. I would have told them that I loved grandma and grandpa more than anything, but I knew I was different than other kids at school. I was the only kid who lived with their grandparents, and it was weird. No one asked. After a few years, I began to think I had imagined all of it. I knew it was strange that to help your dad mow a yard or build a playhouse, you had to go to the basement to "do things." But then again, people had been told and it still happened so what did I know?

I guess looking back mom and Tom were just alike. They were two outcasts of sorts. They were codependents. They were unable to deal with normal day-to-day functions. I think she felt that she'd rather be with him than alone, even during his drunken tirades that I had only seen a few times. I saw him destroy my Beatles drum set by smashing it into the wall at the house before Cross Street. Tom used to burn my toy Army men so he could watch them melt. I saw him put sewing needles and hair from mom's brush in the goldfish tank to watch them strangle to death. I saw him put his foot through that aquarium one night. I started screaming so he taped my mouth with duct tape and told mom not to take it off until he got home. She didn't. She sat on the bed with me all night with my mouth duct-taped until he came back drunk. I know there was a time that I stayed with them and ended up with a huge bruise on my leg when I was about three or four. Mom told grandma and grandpa that Tom spanked me. Later, I overheard someone say that Tom was told to never lay a hand on me again. Of course, that was only referring to getting hit, not molested. I was only there on weekends so I don't know what all he put her through that no one knew about. But she needed him. They both had needs that most people can't understand. She had to have someone to take care of her and to give her attention. He had to touch a little girl to feel some type of control in his life.

In 1987, when I was eighteen, he called and asked for Jolie to come to Oklahoma to visit for the summer, but not Brandon. I heard mom telling him that it wasn't possible. They began to argue about him filing for custody of her. He had only sporadically paid support so I knew that he would never win that fight. However, as the argument became more heated, I decided that it was time I confronted him about what he had done to me over the years. I took the phone from mom and told him that under no circumstances would he ever even think of filing for custody. I informed him that by evening, he would be arrested as I was only a phone call from filing a police report about all of those years in the basement, the garage, and the cars. I told him that people would believe me now. At first he started to argue, and then he tried to test the denial waters. I explicitly told him some of the times I could remember and asked if he wanted that brought out to his family. I told him that how he taught me to give a blow job before I was in kindergarten might not set well with anyone. He listened quietly as I made the threats clear to him. He finally said it would not be necessary and hung up the phone. He had very little contact, even less than before, with Jolie and Brandon from that time forward. He knew that I had told them about their father.

About a year later, we received a call that they had found him and his girlfriend shot in the head in their home. Investigations revealed that he had been a part of an organized child porn ring. Hundreds of thousands of dollars of porn was found in their home amid their decomposing bodies. Apparently, they had been dead about a week before they were found. Rumors surfaced that they may have been facing charges and could testify against the ring. As far as I know, it was classified as a homicide-suicide. There is speculation that it may have been a double homicide. I believe that when Jolie said she saw the devil looking at her dad on Cross Street, she really did.

CHAPTER SEVEN

Greenbriar

The discussion of what he had done to me for seven years, from what I can remember, did not surface again until I was fifteen. I lived with mom by this point, as a result my grandparents dying within a year of each other. I was eleven when I had to move in with her. It was culture shock to say the least. She and Tom had divorced when I was ten. Before they divorced, he had been hired by General Motors. He eventually transferred to Oklahoma. Things were unlike anything I had ever seen at grandmas. Mom slept a lot. She was taking pain killers and nerve pills, along with nose drops. When mom had an occasional job, we had a babysitter named Kay who took great care of our house and us. She was young, but we wouldn't have made it without her and her parents' help during the holidays. My mom's family had drifted out of the picture. They had to separate themselves because they were not strong enough to deal with her. That was my job now or at least that's how I saw it. She would call her brothers and nephews for grocery money weekly. One of them would drop by with a bag full of groceries and give her money. They had learned that by just giving her grocery money, she didn't always make it to the store. After buying her prescriptions, the same ones she had taken for years, the ones she had begun to get her through that painful October of 1969, there wasn't much left for the groceries that we needed. Mom's days were good for her as long as she had the pills to numb her. For us, they were not so good. I began doing my own laundry shortly after moving there at 11 years old. I had seen how grandma did the wash each day, so I worked at it until it turned out right. I had gotten tired of getting up for school without anything clean to wear. There were many days when there was not any toilet paper so the dirty clothes laying beside the toilet were how we wiped our asses. I became disgusted thinking that the clothes I was wearing were probably someone's toilet paper that week. Mom usually wasn't up with us in the mornings. I got the kids up and we grabbed what food we had from the kitchen for breakfast. If the kids didn't want to go to school, I only argued with them until I had to leave. They would then stay until mom got up and found them still at home. Sometimes she took them to school, sometimes she didn't. Mainly, she didn't. I wouldn't go to school if I didn't have lunch money. Mom tried to put me on the free lunch program, but that was worse than death for me in middle school. I never wanted anyone to know how poor we were. I was new to this way of life, so I held onto my old life, the one with grandma and grandpa, if only in my mind. That's how I knew what was wrong with the way we lived. At grandma's, we didn't have to reach into the dirty clothes pile beside the toilet to find something to wipe our ass on. I didn't have to wear wash cloths when I was on my period. Mom didn't see pads as necessary if she was in need of her pills. She had a hysterectomy so she didn't have the same problem as I and didn't need to wear wash cloths. I would stay home from school on these days, too. I eventually got tired of seeing maggots on dirty dishes while I was trying to fix whatever food we had in the house. Before I washed the dishes, every single one that was in the house because mom never did the dishes, I had to take a spatula to get what I called the 'maggot pies" off the plates. Literally, hundreds of maggots on each dish from all of the flies and trash in the house. I had to find a solution, so I washed a plate, a cup, and silverware and hid them in my dresser drawer for me to use. I did the same with a bath towel so I would have something clean to dry with after a shower instead of a mildewed, towel if one could even be found.

On some days, I stayed home from school because I did not have lunch money or pads. Usually one of mom's boyfriends would drop by for, well, for a little while in the bedroom which just made me sick to my stomach. But, I learned to use their drop-ins to my advantage. I would say hello, not usually politely, to whomever once they were surprised to see me home, tell them I needed money for lunch and pads, a ride to the Village Pantry on Madison Avenue, and then a ride to school. They were more than happy to oblige! By the end of the day, mom would be feeling good again. She got that attention she needed, a little money for the doctor's office fee, and for her next prescription. She would be numb again by mid-afternoon, and I would be angry. She always thought she controlled them with sex, but they controlled her with the money and the pills controlled her need for the money. The doctor controlled her need for the pills.

CHAPTER EIGHT

<u>The Ghetto</u>

Her condition wasn't horrible at first. I can look back and see the slow progression. I can remember how at first she just needed to sleep a lot, how she couldn't get awake in the mornings, and then how I could tell she had taken too many pills. We lost our house, the one she and Tom had bought before they divorced, in Greenbriar. We then began a long period of moving from house to house. From 1983 to 1987, we moved seven times, I think. Maybe more. It became almost funny because we occupied five houses in a two block radius near the historic Anderson High School that has since burned to the ground. When rent was due, we just found the next house on the block with a different landlord. I used to tell myself that I wanted to be the one who owned all of the houses so I never had to move. At one point, one of mom's boyfriend's decided that because she owed him money, he could steal my Social Security check which was our only source of income- $350 a month that had to support four people. Rent became due after he took off with the check so we got evicted again. Food was sparse. If we had electricity, we did not have water or heat. After not eating for a couple of days, I confronted mom and told her I didn't care who she had to blow that day but we needed to eat! She told me there was bread in the kitchen so I asked where. When I finally found it squished in a drawer, I opened it and cockroaches crawled out. Infuriated I ran into mom's room and told her. Her response was, "Did they eat it all?" Obviously, the progressive mental and physical downfall was moving faster now.

We first did have houses to live in, but then we were forced to move into a 3-room apartment that was infested with mice and cockroaches. We joked that they were our pets because they ran around the kitchen all day, not just at night when the lights were off. They sometimes crawled on us at night. To this day, I remember the feeling of a cockroach crawling across my arm. I will never forget turning on the kitchen light one night and seeing hundreds of mice on the counters. Old man Jesse actually lived in the apartment but he moved into the basement so we would have someplace to live. Most of our belongings were stored down there. I felt bad for Jesse when it rained because the basement flooded. It didn't seem to bother him that he stepped out of his

rusted cot into four inches of water. I'm sure mom had promised him
something for his trouble, but she was just stringing him along. It was here
that we started losing all of our belongings since they had to be stored in the
basement. We just couldn't get furniture from a three bedroom house into a
three room hole-in-the wall. I would go down there and rearrange my boxes to
keep them off the wet floor. These boxes contained all I had left of my
childhood, the life with grandma and grandpa. Eleven years packed neatly
away in damp cardboard boxes covered in mice feces. We all slept in mom's
queen size bed in the bedroom. It was too big for the room so we couldn't get
into the dressers because the mattresses were pressed up against them.

It was there that I got severely beaten one Sunday morning just a few
weeks before high school started. I was a malnourished white girl, maybe
weighing 80 lbs, living in a predominately black, oppressed neighborhood
where fighting was natural. I had black and mixed friends and did not see
them any differently. But they saw me differently for some reason and made
sure I knew it. I had already learned that backing down was not an option.
Scared or not, I had to stand my ground even if it was just a verbal
confrontation at school, on the street, or at home. After living with mom,
arguments were not a new undertaking. I had been saved in the fight by my
best friend Elaine, who dragged me from under the seven people who found it
necessary to almost kill me: three girls, two boys, and two little kids. The
seven came onto to the porch because another friend of mine, who was black,
asked them graciously to quit harassing me. They retaliated for the request. I
had just gone outside to find my brother, who was about five years old at the
time. We always ran the streets without any boundaries or curfews to be
home, even at five. Mom had gone to work at Hill's Department Store that
morning, one of the only jobs I can remember her having. Two of the girls
began taking out my earrings. I knew I only had one chance so I pushed one
into the door and punched the other. The next thing I remember was being
underneath one of them getting my head pounded into the cement while the
other one was kicking my ribs. The teenage boys held my legs and the two
kids were spitting on me. Nearly unconscious, I felt hands around my ankles
and was being dragged. It was Elaine. She saved me from who knows what
could've happened! Apparently my brother had wandered back to the
apartment and saw what was happening. He ran to Elaine's house. Being five
and not able to communicate well at that age, he simply asked if she was

coming over. She told no but then asked why because we had just been talking on the phone. He calmly replied, "I was just wondering. There are a lot of people beating Taine up right now." Her family called the police as she ran over to the next block to save me.

Elaine and I had been friends since 7th grade when she used to ride her bike by my house and call my mom names shortly after I began living with her. I certainly didn't understand this because that type of thing never happened in North Anderson! Why did she call my mom names and what in the hell were the crabs she was shouting at my mom about? Shortly after the incidents all summer with Elaine, she and I got seated next to one another in Mr. Windlan's science class at Northside Middle School.   We both immediately proclaimed to him that we could not possibly sit next to one another due to our hatred for one another. His reply was, "That is exactly why you are going to stay seated next to each other!" The strategy worked. Before long, we were friends. And not the kind of friendship that ends with hard time. It was the kind that lasted until this day. Mom was infuriated that I had become friends with Elaine. Mom was incredibly prejudiced so Elaine being bi-racial made it worse than even the summer harassment incidents. When I told mom that Elaine was coming by our house to study with me, her reply was, "That little n***** better keep her mouth shut or I will hit her with the car!" I remembered that phrase well because she had called Elaine's mother several times that summer and told her the same thing.

Just one week after the first incident of getting beaten up, one of the seven people showed up to fight again. After her breaking into our apartment, I confronted her. I decided right then that I had to start swinging or she very well could kill me since she out-weighed me by 200 lbs! Elaine, who was also home with me, came out of the other room to see us tearing up most of the living room. I was seated on the girl's lap, punching her in the face. Elaine pulled me from her and tried to stop the fight. The girl then picked up a baseball bat that was in the living room and started swinging at Elaine. It was me this time that was running to her house to get her family. When 9th grade started a week or so later, I walked in with an enormous confidence and a few remaining bruises. One girl started the name-calling during registration. I threw down my books and went toward her. She stopped quickly and said, "I heard you can be a crazy white girl!" I never had another incident.

During the summer of my sophomore year, we moved back to North Anderson on Plum Street. I couldn't bring any friends over because I was humiliated about the way we lived. We were getting poorer, and it showed. Our lives were deteriorating quickly. Mom still had her pills and her doctor though—the only two consistencies in her life. The amount she took was increasing. Sometimes I wish her doctor had to live with us for a week. I wondered how he would feel waking up with cockroaches crawling on him like he was a piece of rotting food. I wonder how angry it would make him wiping his ass on a shirt his little sister had to wear. I bet he never had to eat cereal without milk. I bet he never opened a loaf of bread, the only food in the house to eat, and saw roaches running out. I wonder how it would make his skin crawl to turn on a light a see a hundred mice scurrying off your stove. I wonder if during his childhood, he ever had to choose between having electricity to see with, or gas for warm showers. It became natural for us to have one or the other utilities, but rarely both. If we had Kool-Aid, we didn't have running water to make it. Our favorite food became the generic Velveeta cheese block from a church food pantry. We were without a telephone for the majority of the time. But he was a licensed doctor, with a nice car, nice family, food in his refrigerator. He had his thriving drug practice, and "payment arrangements" with mom. She had her addiction.

It was in 1984 on Plum Street, when I was fifteen, that mom and I were in yet another shouting contest. I was an angry teenager, taken from my way of life, and thrown into hell. That's when I slipped about her not protecting me from Tom. She began to cry almost immediately. She got quiet, and under her breath asked a question that she had known the answer to for years: Was that true? I said, "Hell yes it was true. That's why it kept going on, because you thought I was lying?" All of those years had passed, and I thought I had imagined it all: the abuse, the talk with her, everything. She asked again what had happened in that musty basement. I told her and did not spare her feelings when I described the events that took place in that dungeon. Nor did I leave out any of the details when I told her about when it happened even after they were divorced, and he was home from Oklahoma for a weekend. I had spared her feelings as much as could when I was young, but not his time. I told her about having to jack him off in the garage after she went to sleep. I told her how he would make me come inside so he could touch me after she left with Jolie and Brandon for the store. Her only reply through the tears was that she could barely have sex with him after I had told her what he had been doing. I knew right then that she had believed me the first time but didn't have the strength to get away from him. After all, she had to have suspected it or she wouldn't have asked when I was five years old. I often had wondered how she stayed married for another 5 years and had another baby after the first talk of it. But, there's an easy answer to that question: he had income even if it was only occasionally, and she needed the money for the pills and doctor.

CHAPTER NINE

The Doctor

I went to see mom on June 3, 2000. I hadn't seen her since Christmas. She was lying on the bed in the living room with the heating pad on as she had for as long as I could remember. Her back was purplish-blue, discolored from the heating pad that had almost cooked her skin. She was going through withdrawal again. She kept telling me she didn't want us to ever see her go through the involuntary shaking from her degenerative back disease. That was another false diagnosis by the doctor she worshipped. The truth was that mom did not have any back muscles from lying down for the past ten years. I don't ever remember mom sitting up, except in one picture that was taken after Jolie was born. She began to tell me about all of the people who watch her through the windows, or try to sabotage her car. I ignored that as I had for the past few years. It was some type of paranoia she had been going through. In addition to the Xanax addiction, I knew mom had some form of mental illness along with what I believed to be anorexia. If she had a headache, she took a pain pill without food. Then she would tremble from the pain pill, so she would take a Xanax and tell people that it was due to her back disease. Then the two combined would make her throw up. If she did manage to eat that day, she usually got diarrhea. This would make her weak so she would say that her blood sugar was too low. She would then drink a Root Beer or Pepsi, and the caffeine on an empty stomach would set in motion the trembling again. Then it was another Xanax. At fifty-one years old, mom was losing hearing in one ear. I didn't believe her at first and thought it was another attempt at getting attention. I noticed that when I called her every other week or so, her speech was becoming more slurred. She talked sometimes like she had suffered a stroke. I would get off the phone with her and say that she was "zoned out again." We had been trying to get her away from her doctor for years. My sister volunteered to take her to Colorado with her. Mom's only answer was that she couldn't leave her doctor because he was the only one who knew what was wrong with her. That translated to the fact that she couldn't leave the only one would give her unlimited pills, let her diagnose her own illnesses, all while using her for sex, which she had told me about fifteen years before. I had talked to several agencies where mom lived to see if I could get her involuntarily admitted. The answer was always the same: only if she is a danger to herself or someone else, then we would need a doctor's referral. That was the whole problem-the doctor. He was the only one mom would see. We could not tear her away from him. I asked mom several times to come to Bloomington to a hospital, to be near me so I could get her real help. Again, she would say "but how will I get back here to the doctor?" I refused to live near mom because she was allowing her doctor to kill her slowly. He should have been the responsible one to monitor her, to limit her pill usage, to send her to the right facilities to get help for her mental deterioration. But he wasn't. He was there to prescribe toxic doses of medicine that was slowly killing her. She had been told to come through the back door of his clinic so other patients wouldn't see her and that DEA had undercover officers all over. His waiting room always had over fifty people waiting. The parking lot was full. He worked into the night prescribing one script after another for a simple office fee and whatever else he could get from desperate women.

The day I left her, she barely had the strength to walk me to the car. I had to deal with the smell of rotting food in the house since she had stomach spasms and could not get up easily. I could feel and see the knots forming in her stomach as she went through the withdrawal from the Xanax and the pain killer. It was like a scene from an alien movie watching these fist-like spasms in her stomach reaching out. Her arms were flying outward uncontrollably. I had to sit and watch her go through what the doctor had helped her to do to herself. Mom was a skeleton. Her skin hung on what bones she had. Her hair was matted with a layer of crust. It looked like it had crumbs of food in it. Her mouth was pasty, her skin white. She was in a lingerie- type shirt that hadn't been washed in who knows how long. Mom smelled liked a person who lived in a sewer, and I could hardly stand to touch her. It scared me. She wanted me to hold her. I tried but had to keep pulling away like she had some disease I didn't want to contract. What was I going to do? I was sick about it. Then mom shocked me. She said to get Jolie home so she could see her one last time. I told her not to talk that way. I wanted to act as though it was bad for her to speak of her death, but really I was terrified.

Mom started telling me that her doctor had stopped seeing her because of her "condition." She was furious. I was furious yet relieved. He kept her addicted to the point that she had to go to emergency rooms in every county in central Indiana to get more pills if he was out of town. Occasionally, he would tell her that he had to wait another few days before he could prescribe again, as though three hundred Xanax month was not enough. That was a great way to cover his ass, while she risked having a withdrawal-induced stroke or heart attack. Mom had told me of times he sent her out the back door of his office because the undercover narcotic agents were in his waiting room. He knew she was a walking billboard for drug addiction, and being her dealer, he had to protect himself and his illegal "medical" practice. He had even asked mom what she had been doing because the FBI had looked at her records. He knew exactly what she was doing. She would buy Xanax for $5 a pill on the street if he couldn't legally prescribe her more for a period. He had even told her not to buy on the street because she didn't know what she would get. Yet, he still prescribed. He had been notified that mom was filling scripts from numerous pharmacies all over central Indiana. Yet he still prescribed. He was told she was selling pills that he prescribed. Yet, he still prescribed. I knew mom had lost too much weight. I didn't know how much she weighed, but I knew it was obviously in a dangerously low range. I had asked her what the doctor said about her weight, even though I didn't care a damn thing about what he said. Apparently, there had never been any discussion of it even though she was skeletal. Yet, he still prescribed.

I drove back to southern Indiana from Anderson that day thinking, crying. I just didn't know how to get her away from his grip. When I arrived home, I got a call from Jolie who said that mom had sent her a letter about her funeral requests. Jolie was scared, and thought it was time to do something drastic. Ironically, Brandon had called about her as well. I told them that we all had to be in agreement and that I would go back to get mom. Against her wishes if I had to do it that way. We all agreed that now was the time because she was mad at the doctor for not seeing her anymore. I had made hundreds of calls in the past to find her help. Everyone wanted to admit her, with insurance and a referral from her doctor. We hit a dead end everywhere we turned. I even had called about getting a court order for inpatient treatment. I was told that unless she was a danger to herself or others, it would not be ordered. Dying a slow death from prescription drug addiction did not fall under that category. After the decision was made among the three of us, I called mom. I told her that we would help, but not by giving her money. She had to come to Bloomington, go to the hospital, and do whatever they said. Strangely, she agreed. She had never agreed before. I started making arrangements, and I went back two days later to get her. She was relieved just being out of that house. She was nervous because I had made her an appointment with a crisis care doctor in an addictions unit. That night, she went through night sweats and diarrhea. She kept saying that she didn't want anyone to know that she was in an addictions unit. She insisted she was not an addict; she just needed her medication for her back disease and her ear imbalance. We arrived the next morning at the hospital for what I had hoped would be a turning point in all of our lives.

CHAPTER TEN

<u>The Hospital</u>

Upon arriving at the Crisis Care door, I noticed the jail-like appearance. I had to call the desk, somewhere behind a locked steel door, using an intercom. We were asked if we had an appointment and who we were there to see. After confirming that our visit was legitimate, we were allowed to enter. A staff quickly responded after seeing mom. Within minutes they had her hooked up to IV's, had taken her vitals, and began filling out the paperwork to get Medicaid assistance. The doctor would not accept Medicaid due to governmental oversight-only insurance, primarily GM, and cash- so he would never sign her application for it.

I stood there in amazement, watching the staff scurry around trying to get her intake completed. I couldn't believe that so much was being completed the first moments after we walked through the door. After all, mom had been going to the same doctor for twenty-five years and never received this much true medical care. I thought of all of the years of fighting with her to change doctors. And there we were, away from Anderson, away from the other addicts, away from the doctor. I felt for the first time in my life that everything would be okay now.

After a few minutes they told me, in a grave tone, that she weighed 83 pounds and was not sure how long she would make it but to remain hopeful. I just stared at them. What did this mean? They began explaining that mom was in serious state of malnutrition. I had always suspected bulimia or anorexia. I knew that her doctor and his so-called staff could not have been blind to her skeletal appearance. Yet, he did nothing for decades except feed her the pills that deprived her of appetite, feeling, and life while depriving us of a mother, care, and love. I guess I never wanted to admit that she could die. But at this point, it became a reality. The doctor told me that before he could treat the addiction and possible mental illness, he had to treat the immediate medical problems. She had to be weaned from her pills, and she had to eat.

During the intake process, mom held tight onto her purse. I knew there must be Xanax in it or she wouldn't have a death grip on it. That's ironic. Death had a grip on her and she couldn't let go of her purse! I forcibly took it from her. I wanted to comfort her, but I had to be strong. She had to see that she was not going to wear me down. I was not going to allow her to turn back now. We were 60 miles from the doctor…the furthest I had ever gotten her. I wonder if he ever had to go through what I was being forced to endure. Mom was shaking, crying for her medication, holding onto me. For the first time ever, she had a hold on me and not her pills. Each hour, another staff member would arrive to explain what they would be doing with mom's case. A Medicaid representative was finishing off the paperwork so that mom could get the treatment she needed when a nutritional expert arrived to find out what mom would eat. I was impressed by the promptness of everybody, yet it was just another clue that she was in a critical situation.

As mom undressed, I saw the skin that hung on her bones. There was not any muscle left. Every vertebra in her back stuck out, her tailbone was raw from her jeans rubbing the ends of bone. Her back had purple splotches under the skin. Mom barely had any strength, mentally or physically by the end of the day. Even though they had to wean her from her pills with another form of medication, she was being forced to deal with the immediate circumstances. Instead of being allowed to numb herself into drug-induced sleep as she was accustomed, she had to face us—the ones who loved her and the ones trying to save her life.

The next two weeks were exhausting trying to maintain my work schedule while running to the hospital every chance I had and completing the paperwork to get her government housing once she was released. I hoped the chance of having her own house would give her hope. I had begun guardianship proceedings with a local attorney to make sure that I could keep her in Bloomington when she was released. For once, I felt like I could truly help her. Before, I would never go to Anderson to take her to the doctor nor send her money. I knew that the money would go to him, the doctor dealer who controlled her life. When I visited, I took her groceries instead…food that she would never eat. But I never could truly help her.

Mom went through a series of procedures. The Crisis Care doctor ran a complete set of tests to determine what, if anything, was really wrong with her health aside from the apparent. It was determined that she had little wrong with her physically. There was nothing except age-related, minor issues. I had always known there was some type of mental illness, but it had never been diagnosed. Mom would not seek mental help, unless it was a way for her to get her pills—the pills that he said she had to have. He usually diagnosed her without any tests. He fed her false information about her health, and raked in the charges for every office visit in one way or another. It is my presumption that one primary reason GM left Anderson was due to medical costs, there as everyone knew that the doctor would sign paperwork for sick leave and collect insurance money while getting the employees doped up on their cocktail of choice. During a visit, a patient could just tell him what she/he wanted, even picking up for relatives.

Within days mom had been put through more tests than ever before. It was determined that aside from a gall bladder problem, an operation for which she was not strong enough to endure, she needed nutrients. It was decided that a feeding tube would be placed so that her body would be force-fed. Mom was still begging for her pills, saying that this was all wrong. I think she was starting to realize the seriousness of her condition. Yet, she still would not admit to being addicted. She would still say, even after seeing the test results, that it was a conspiracy against her. She would state adamantly that *her* doctor was only doctor who knew what was really wrong with her. I told her that I was no longer going to argue about these issues. Once he had been notified by her so-called friends, also by the dealers and addicts that were under his care, or abuse as it was, why did he not call? She had been under his care for twenty-five years, yet not one phone call to check on her condition. "Where is he now?" I would ask her. She did not have any answers. I did. He was still in practice with a hundred more people just like mom trusting him with their lives.

After the tube was placed, the next few days were critical. She had constant diarrhea, sometimes having no control at all. Mom always had bowel problems for as long as I can remember. The packets of Imodium I found after her death proved to me that she knew it was a problem. Along with causing herself to throw up each day, I don't know how she made it as long as she did. Looking back at the medications my grandmother, also a patient of the same doctor, took daily, I would guess that mom had been born addicted in some form. It has been said that grandma took Phenobarbital, a highly addictive drug, while she was pregnant with mom. I had been told over the years that mom screamed non-stop from the day she was born with nothing ever found to be the cause. Mom was just treated, given medication, and sent home from his office. A pattern that would continue for the rest of her life.

CHAPTER ELEVEN

<u>Grandma</u>

Grandma had to keep track of her medications by making a list. Each time she took a pill, it was noted on the paper that was taped inside of the cabinet door. I never thought that grandma was in poor health really. She just seemed really old for being sixty-four. She did not drive and seldom would she ever leave the house. I would say she had agoraphobia, which mom had started signs of, too. Both of them would have an anxiety attack or diarrhea when they left the house. As long as the car stayed on the path to the doctor's office, the panic attacks didn't happen for either of them. There was an occasional trip to Kmart on Sundays to get ham sandwiches in a bag or to Kentucky Fried Chicken with grandpa and me, which didn't seem to adversely affect her. Of course, we were usually home within an hour. She always made our dinners from scratch, rolling out the dough for noodles and dumplings and other favorites of our family. Since we lived in the center of town and with such a large family, you just never knew who would stop in for dinner. Grandma had always cooked enough to feed the neighborhood since it was all relatives from both sides. I never knew what fast-food really was until I moved in with mom. I didn't even have a pizza for the first time until I was almost eleven. Grandma was a stickler for cleanliness. The house was spotless. I was spotless. I was not even allowed to make my Sunday evening trips to Dairy Queen without at least a spit-cleaning from her hankie on my face, which my aunt tried to do to me until I was about thirty. Grandma's road trips were mainly to the doctor. Either grandpa took her, or Aunt Florence did after she had prosthetic legs. On one of those trips, she did not return. I was only 11 years old at the time, but I remember the details vividly. You remember the details that change your life forever.

It had been one year and four days since grandpa had walked to the ambulance that morning. Grandma had gone to the doctor's office for a routine visit. Most visits to him were too routine. It was the first time I had persuaded her and mom that I could baby-sit for Jolie and Brandon by myself. It was Veteran's Day, November 11th, and school was closed. I had never been allowed to stay alone at home, or at moms, let alone baby-sit. But since grandpa had died, many things were different. I had started doing some grocery shopping on my own. Grandma bought me a cart, like old Mrs. Whitaker's. Until then, I wasn't even allowed to cross Broadway. Now I was doing the shopping with my cart. On November 10th, mom picked me up from grandma's. The plan was to go to mom's house overnight, then she would take Jolie, Brandon, and I back to grandma's the next morning. Mom wanted to put in some job applications so she needed me to watch the kids.

While mom was there picking me up, an event happened that forced me to believe in all of the superstitions that the family spoke of. Before that day, I would turn off my hearing when the talk of the "signs of death" were mentioned. Indian legends always seemed to find a place in the conversations in the family. Since Mounds Indians had once lived on the soil that Anderson was built on, it kept the imaginations alive. I often say that the city is actually cursed along with everyone in it.

I had taken my sister and brother into my room to play my radio while mom and grandma talked. Mom was probably was asking grandma for money as she usually did. Grandma would often give it to her because she knew that mom would just ask grandpa. But since grandpa had passed away, grandma was a little more defiant with mom when it came to money. After a few minutes, I heard grandma ask me a question from the dining room. I came out from my room and smelled an overwhelming, almost sickening, smell of flowers. It wasn't like the fragrance from the wild honeysuckle on the house. It was a pungent floral odor that filled the dining and living room. Grandma's face was pasty white as she asked me again, "Did you spill perfume in your room?" I froze and looked at mom. I knew what they were going to say. I knew what it meant. I had heard the family talk about it for years. I replied weakly, "No, I don't have any perfume out." Funeral flowers. The house was filled with the smell of a funeral home. I knew the smell well coming from such an old family. It seems like every month someone passed away. I tried to get it out of my mind. I was scared. It wasn't just talk that I overheard. I could smell it before they even said anything. Now, I had to get it out of my mind! We left to go to mom's house, but the thought stayed with me. I couldn't talk about. I didn't want to even think about it. Once we got to mom's, I started playing with my siblings and put it to rest, or so I thought.

Mom left that evening so we had a babysitter, Kay. I loved Kay. She was young and cool and took part in our lives. She had a 70's something black Monte Carlo with leather seats. I had never heard a stereo so loud in a car, but

I hated her rock music. I had been raised on country and rock hurt my ears. I was just starting to listen to disco. Mom listened to pop. When Kay was around, I didn't want to go back to grandmas. Kay understood things about eleven year olds. Her family always helped out during the holidays as times got progressively worse. That night, strange things began to happen. Sounds, feelings that couldn't be explained. And then, Grandma started calling on the phone. She would ask if I had my coat with me. I would reply sharply that yes, I did have my coat. She would ask if she gave me money. Again, I replied, "Yes." She said she loved me and just wanted to make sure I was all right. I knew that grandma didn't really like me going to moms. She usually called when I was there. But this was different. She called several times, always asking me the same things, telling me she loved me. I wish I would have understood. I wish I would have had a conversation with her. I was at moms and Kay was there, and we were having fun. I didn't want to keep getting bothered by the phone calls.

The next day, the eleventh, Veteran's Day, mom took me as planned back home to grandmas. She left to put in job applications or so she said. My brother, sister, and I were playing in my room. I felt a little uneasy about being in charge for the first time, being alone. I had almost forgotten about the previous night. Our house scared me a little so I turned on the eight track cassette player in the dining room. I don't think I was ever allowed to do that by myself, but I wanted to show off since my brother and sister were there. I went back into my room. Suddenly, the music either turned down or off. I immediately got scared. The hair stood up on my arms and neck. I could barely walk out to see what had happened to the music. As I went into the dining room, the phone rang interrupted the deafening silence, scaring me more.

"Hello," I said quietly.
"Where's your mom?" the other voice asked.
 "I don't know," I said.
"We have to find your mom," the voice said firmly.
"Where's my grandma," I asked.
"We have to find your mom."
The voice was my grandmother's sister, Florence, who had taken her to the doctor.
"Put grandma on the phone." I demanded.

I felt like this went on for several minutes, back and forth. I knew she should not be calling instead of grandma. I knew something was terribly wrong.

"We have to find your mom because your grandma had a stroke in the doctor's office. She's on the way to the hospital!"

I froze. Then I started to tremble. The tears began to fill my eyes. I knew if I blinked the tears would roll down my young cheeks showing my weakness, my fear. I couldn't cry now. Not while I was in charge. I didn't realize then that my whole life was about to be turned upside down, inside out. From this day forward, I would almost be in charge for the rest of my youth. I had to find mom quickly. I hung up, got out the phonebook, and started calling the places I thought she would be applying for work. All of the concerned voices kept saying that they had not seen anyone by that name that day. I had almost given up when I decided to call her house. Maybe she went home for something. She did. She went home to sleep. As she answered, I became infuriated that she was there, yet thankful she was on the other end of the line with me.

"Mom?" I firmly asked.

"Yeah?" She replied from her sleepy daze.

"Grandma had a stroke at the doctor. You come get me right now," I ordered.

Within minutes, I saw her car pull through the front yard, not even the driveway. We raced to the hospital. It seemed like just yesterday when we had made this same trip with grandpa. I didn't have to fight about this trip, though. She took me immediately. Grandma was all I had left.

I walked into her room. All eyes turned toward me and arms began to reach out. I didn't want anyone but grandma. I pushed past everyone and went to her bedside. I remember them telling her that I was there. She reached out with her left hand to grab mine. Her right side was paralyzed and she could not speak. She managed to get my hand and place it across her heart. Her hands and skin were always so soft. She kept squeezing it and tapping it against her limp body, trying to say she loved me. The words were slurred, but I understood them. She kept trying to talk but I'm not sure if she realized why she couldn't speak. I tried to be strong and listen to what everyone was telling me. But it was too much. I had to leave. I had to leave right then. I took off running from the room and tried to get on the elevator before it closed. Someone grabbed me. I think it was my Uncle Tim. He held onto me so tight I couldn't breathe. I couldn't have breathed even if he hadn't been squeezing me so tight. After a few moments of trying to compose myself, I went back into the room and listened to the adults. I knew if I acted like a child, they wouldn't let me stay, just like they wouldn't let me see grandpa. I heard them say that she had been asking to be buried in a white robe, and had made gestures with one hand like she wanted a robe that crossed. I couldn't bear to hear that so I went into the hallway again. It had only been a little over a year, and I was going through this again. But this time, I would be losing the only home I had ever known. Little did I know then, but the rest of my life I would be searching for that lost family and sense of home I had known for only eleven short years.

Grandma had been given a steroid shot for an ailment of some sort I was told. The doctor, the same doctor, gave her a steroid shot with high blood pressure. As she was leaving the doctor's office, she suffered a cerebral hemorrhage. She never recovered. She died a month later in an Indianapolis hospital from surgery-related pneumonia. Grandma was a short, plump woman with frail, soft skin that turned purple from any touch. I would always play with the flabby skin under her arm, until I realized how much it bruised her. She said it didn't hurt, but I never knew for sure. She always swore pant-suits that were bought from Mr. Ramsey, the door-to door salesman. I don't think she ever wore the same suit twice. Mr. Ramsey would come to our door once a month with his boxed goods that were bound with rubber bands. He would carefully un-tie the long skinny cardboard boxes, while chewing his Dentyne gum. He was always dressed in suit, with a hat on his head. Mr. Ramsey reminded me of George, the old man at the store who always talked with grandpa and me. He always smelled like the cinnamon from his chewing gum. On my birthdays, he would give me a half-dollar for my grandma to keep for me. I don't know what happened to the jar she kept them in. They disappeared like everything else in the house. Like everything else in my life. He would shake my hand, slipping a piece of gum into mine, with a sly smile on his face like it was a secret just between him and me. He kept grandma, and her sisters, well dressed.

Seeing grandma that next month with her jaws sunken from not having her dentures in, eyes with dark circles around them, beautiful, perfect snow-white hair shaved down to the scalp, tubes in her mouth and nose, gowns that barely covered her bruised body, and that gurgling sound from the breathing apparatus made me queasy. I can still smell the odor of old cafeteria food, sickness, and death from that hospital. I lived with mom from Veteran's Day on. I can remember how some my great-aunts would say that the doctor killed grandma. The ones that didn't go to him, of course. It scared me. I didn't understand how he could have killed her. It wasn't until I learned the dangers of steroid shots and blood pressure later in life that I understood. It wasn't long before I realized that even though grandma was taken from me suddenly, mom would die slowly from the same cause.

CHAPTER TWELVE

<u>Bedford</u>

Mom had started looking better than I had seen her look in fifteen years in the two weeks she had been at the hospital. I started to let my guard down, telling myself that the worst had passed. I couldn't believe that the whole process had reversed itself. I would walk in and there was mom, with make-up on, hair washed, with new clothes. I can remember when the way she looked was important to her. She was like grandma that way. It had been years though, since she truly cared. All of the family had a certain appearance to uphold, it seemed. They were a well-known family in the town so maybe the status was important. Maybe it was just the era. We weren't rich by any means, but everyone in the family had a position. I was proud to be a part of that family. Grandpa was one of the most well-known and liked men I ever knew. He was a leader, a patriarch, a provider. It came natural to him.

I was thankful that we had gotten her help in time. We began to look at long-term care facilities that accepted Medicaid. The real doctor said that she would be home by Christmas, and it was a long way to recovery. In some ways, I knew she never would fully recover. I had hope though that maybe, just maybe, that we would get a chance to be a family. The doctor always stood between us as a family. She needed him, not us. She loved us, but she couldn't take care of us. She could not even take care of herself. I chose a facility in Bedford, Indiana so that I could be close to her. I started looking into buying a house there so that she could live with me until government housing was available once she was released. I knew that I had to get her on her feet and give her a life here so that she would never return to the filthy hell in which she lived in Anderson. I had to keep her away from him more than anything else.

On that drive to the facility, I could tell she was scared. We had talked that day like we had never talked before. There were so many places I wanted to show her. I kept telling her about the big Christmas we would have…all of us together. I should have seen that there was not true excitement for that, for she had already told me that every time she closed her eyes, she saw a casket. I, of course, ignored those statements as I always had. I tried to give her hope. I tried to give me hope.

Brandon was coming home that night and Jolie in a few short days. That did excite her. She kept asking when Brandon would meet us there. I kept telling her that by the time we had gotten settled in, he would be home from Ft. Leonard Wood. She always wanted all of us by her, but the need for the pills—the cravings and the withdrawals—controlled her life. We got her settled in as much as possible. He and I ran to Wal-Mart to get her some personal items that would make her room more comfortable. We got a picture collage so that she could have our pictures with her. We got her a new quilt. It had been years since she had slept on clean bed clothes. We were excited at the chance of getting our mom to a state that she could function as a mom, as a human, not as a drug addict living like an animal in filth. However, that did not happen. It was two days after admitting her to the facility that she passed away in her sleep, between 4 and 6 am on Sunday morning. I know the exact time of death was 4:52 am. I woke from a sound sleep and wondered why I had awakened so abruptly at that time. Not paying attention to the feeling, I drifted back off into sleep only to be awakened by yet another phone call that would send my life into yet another new direction.

It was over for her and us. Final. No chance at getting our mom a somewhat normal life. No possibilities of her making it through a day without a pill. We now have to live with the memories of when we were little, before the progression began to roll downhill full-speed. I can remember good times with her. I hold onto to those memories because they were so few. Fifty-one years old, in a nursing home with Alzheimer's patients, unable to control bowel movements, a feeding tube permanently inside her stomach, eighty-six pounds now, and a funeral. Those are my memories now.

CHAPTER THIRTEEN

The Lessons

Life has many lessons to teach. The question is whether or not we will learn from all of the struggles, pain, and grief, so that when we feel the happiness, and see the sunshine, we'll appreciate it. Losing everyone I have ever loved has taught me to take nothing for granted. I live each day as if there will not be a tomorrow. My experiences, whether tragic, unfortunate, or blessed were placed before me to give me strength, to give me goals, and to make me as good a person as I can be. Most importantly, I was put on this Earth to love. It would have been easy to shut my feelings off over the years, to never give or receive love, to be pessimistic about life and its challenges. Instead, I have chosen to analyze my history, study the lessons set before me, and prepare for my future, whatever that might be. Lessons are continually part of our lives. Painful challenges have recently been laid before me that have sent my life once again into a new direction. Although I cannot see the reasons right now, I'm sure I will eventually.

The basement on Cross Street and the events that began there, laid the foundation for who I am today. Unlike many who suffer sexual abuse, I do not hold any grudges against him. He was a disturbed soul who met his fate. Unfortunately, his two children have to live knowing what type of man he was. Even though many wonder how mom could have let it go on like she did, she was faced with great internal struggles that consumed her. I was given the challenge to overcome, to forgive. It was the first of many in my life.

The death of my grandparents, my caretakers, marked the end of my childhood at eleven. Most people either have good or bad memories of their childhood years. For me, there is a clear division between the good and bad. Although I was enduring much more than my grandparents ever knew, and it wasn't perfect by any means, my childhood memories with them are filled with big family dinners and old traditional holidays. Those good times overshadow what happened in the basement when I visited my mom. The basement events were only preparing me to become who I had to be and the strength I would need.

Moving in with mom taught me responsibility. I had to become a caretaker when grandma and I were alone for her last year. But that year with grandma, going to the store with her lists, being home when she said, and helping her was setting me up for what I was about to undertake. Even at eleven years old, I felt I had a responsibility to raise Jolie and Brandon. I loved my mother, but I could see she was not in any position to provide the physical stability they needed, let alone the emotional nurturing. I always have strived to keep the three of us together as a family, no matter what. Mom tried in her own ways, and I feel compelled to do the same. Somehow I knew at a young age that I had to stay away from drugs and not get pregnant because it was up to me to change the trajectory of our lives. I knew I did not want to end up in a perpetual cycle of poverty and addiction, although mom's family was not like her. I had the chance to see how life should be living with grandma and grandpa and the Maxwell family, even just in eleven short years. I knew I had to take care of Jolie and Brandon the best I could, mainly by being the parent, to ensure they could lead productive lives outside of Anderson.

I knew a real shot at college was not a possibility, although I did attend Ball State for a failed attempt at a Psychology major. I joined the National Guard at twenty years old so I could experience life somewhere else, gain perspective, breathe. I eventually moved to Bloomington with my girlfriend and, at twenty-five, I was able to attend Indiana University for my Bachelor's degree. I quickly decided that I loved Sociology and hoped one day I would be able to teach, although I had no actual plan to make that happen. I was accepted into the Police Cadet Program at IU and worked on campus as a Police Officer for many years while also managing retail loss prevention. Eventually, I was able to open a small café/bar and then a larger restaurant, but the recession in 2008 changed all of that. At the time, I also owned several rental homes and had flipped a house. The recession once again derailed my plans, my life, as I lost almost everything.

As usual, the universe certainly has a strange way of putting those lost ones on track even though it can't be seen at the time. I jumped at the opportunity of becoming part-time adjunct faculty at Ivy Tech Community College teaching Life Skills. When I saw the ad in the newspaper I thought to myself if anyone has skills for life, it's me! Finding a great love in teaching, I set out on a path to return to school for a Master's degree in Adult Education.

I accepted a full-time faculty position at Ivy Tech in Indianapolis, moved from Bloomington, earned an Assistant Professorship, and once again returned to school after a few years—finally for Sociology post-graduate work. This allowed me to finally teach in the discipline rather than just in an administrative/life skills position. Mainly, I hoped Sociology would help me put the pieces together of every event that shaped me. I thought that if I could understand drug addiction, mental illness, and sexual abuse, my life would have true meaning. Education for me was not just a means for better income and stability, it was for actual understanding which brought about peace. Using my fee remission at Ivy Tech, I also completed an HR Management certificate program as I worked my way into the federal government while still teaching in an adjunct capacity once again. In addition, I am now also a licensed realtor which fulfills a personal goal from my teenage years when we were constantly being evicted, and I wanted to be the one who owned the houses.

While my life was coming together, my sister's and brother's lives were, too. Jolie has been able to travel overseas, finished college, and works in the medical field in Florida. I forced Brandon to join the Army as a firefighter after high school because I knew that was the best path for him. It led him to being a civilian firefighter for the federal government for the past twenty years. He has three wonderful children and is a fantastic father. One niece is talking about being a doctor, and my nephew is a terrific athlete. All three are loving, sweet, smart, and kind, beautiful souls. Our family life trajectory was certainly altered in so many enormous ways. They will never know how different their lives could have been.

Goals, perseverance, and ambition led me to life-long learning and self-actualization. I believe that my life is about the experiences and the journey so I must be here for some actual purpose. Mom must have been my purpose. She was not an involved parent, but somehow we knew she loved us. It's hard to imagine a mother doing some of the things our mom did us, the life she forced us to endure, but through it all I realized that her problems began long ago. She was a lost soul that never found her way in this world. She became an astrologer and tried use psychic abilities to understand *her* world. She had a ninth grade education, but taught herself more about Native American spiritualism than I ever could. It was due to her pain, her emotional suffering, that she was able to gain the insight she needed just to survive daily.

And through it all she was a survivor! It took strength for her to live the way she did. To me, her death was a triumph because she finally found peace.

It has been difficult for each of us in our own ways. Even though we were not close to her, there has been a dynamic void in our lives. It took me three years to erase her number from my cell phone just because I needed to see it there. My anger toward her has subsided now that I have reached a level of understanding. Time does heal. I can now just shake my head at the time she forged my paychecks from working as the Easter Bunny at the Castleton Mall, or when I almost got prosecuted for bad checks that she had stolen out of my box of bank checks after I got home from basic training. I am sure my sister is no longer mad at her for getting to the gas station on a visit to Anderson, only to find mom had stolen the money from her purse. She had to call me to charge it so they would not call the police. I think Brandon has forgiven her for taking his paychecks from working on a farm one summer in high school without him knowing. She convinced the farmer that she needed gas money or he could not come to work. He thought he was getting paid at the end of the summer since he was not getting checks. What a wild life we had with her! I can still hear Elaine chuckling and shaking her head when we tell stories, now to her grandchildren, saying "Ole Deb!"

We have to believe that she was finally taken from this Earth, this world, and relieved of her physical and emotional pain, to reach a higher goal than she was able to achieve here. She is buried in Anderson next to my grandparents. Although it is not close to him, it is the same cemetery where my father is buried. I believe that in the end, it's what she wanted. She is reunited with him and, just as a child needs protection, she has returned to her parents. I feel a stronger connection to her now than I did while she was here. It is because I now understand the dynamics of her life, and death, that I have reached forgiveness and a level of love that I never had before. I'll end with the inscription on her headstone: "Rest in Peace, Mom."